The Highlights Book of
Things to Do
OUTDOORS

HIGHLIGHTS PRESS
HONESDALE, PENNSYLVANIA

CONTENTS

HOW TO USE THIS BOOK

It's completely up to you how you use this book. You can start at the beginning, flip to the end and work backward, or jump to any page that inspires you. You can also complete the activities based on how you're feeling. If you feel like experimenting, you might choose to flip to the chapter called "Super Science." If you love animals, you can start with the "Amazing Animals" chapter. If you are short on time, try our "6 Quick Challenges" at the start of every chapter. The great thing is, you don't have to worry about what to do. We've given you lots of ideas to try out. If you're having trouble picking an activity, pick one at random and give it a go— you can always switch crafts or games at any time. If an activity inspires you to do something completely different, try that instead! And keep in mind that you can always alter the activities to fit you and where you live. Remember that this book is about having fun outdoors in the way that *you* want.

SAFETY FIRST!

Some activity prompts in this book suggest that you handle hot objects, research subjects online, or ask people questions. Make sure you check with a parent, a teacher, or another grown-up first, and always have an adult present when using sharp or hot items. We have noted when it is necessary to have a grown-up help you. The most important bit of advice we have for using this book, however, is not to worry about perfection. Be creative! Make mistakes and try again! Most of all, enjoy yourself.

Look up some of the wild animals that live in your area. Draw your favorite one here.

Quick Challenges
AMAZING ANIMALS

Write a poem about your favorite animal. Use as many words as you can that start with the first letter in the animal's name (for example, if you pick a tiger, try to use lots of words that start with the letter *T*).

_____

_____

_____

_____

If you could have a tail like an animal, which animal's tail would you want? Draw yourself with a tail here.

Turn some recycled materials—like paper plates and string—into fun animal masks to use while playing outside.

Practice animal noises by yourself or with a friend.

Design an outdoor pet paradise—like an awesome doghouse, a fantastic horse stable, or a sweet bunny hutch—and draw it here.

Build a Birdbath

Just like people, birds need clean water for drinking and bathing. Make a safe spot for birds to take a dip with this DIY birdbath.

You Need

- 2 to 3 terra-cotta pots of slightly different sizes that can be stacked upside down to form a tower
- 1 terra-cotta saucer or pot base
- Waterproof adhesive such as rubber cement or construction adhesive
- Water
- Nontoxic outdoor acrylic paints (optional)
- Paintbrushes (optional)

1. If you want, decorate the outsides of your pots and your saucer with your paint. Let dry completely.

2. Turn your largest pot upside down, and then stack your next largest pot upside down on top of it. If you want, you can have an adult help you add adhesive in between the pots for extra stability. If using a third pot, stack it upside down on the tower, too. This will be the base for your birdbath.

3. Have an adult help you use your adhesive to glue the saucer on top of your pot tower. Let dry.

4. Pick a good, flat spot for your birdbath. This can be in a yard, on a balcony, or in a local park or garden (just make sure to get permission first).

5. Once your birdbath is set in its spot, add some water into the saucer. Keep watch and see if some birds come to have a drink or make a splash!

Use this space to sketch some designs for your birdbath.

FEATHERY FUN

Use this space to keep a log of the birds that visit your birdbath.
Note the different types of birds you see, which types of birds
visit most often, and more.

Design some beautiful feathers for a bird. They can be based on the feathers you see on real birds or totally made up!

Tracking Animals

Animals are often good at keeping themselves hidden—but one way to tell if they've been near is to look at the tracks, or paw and footprints, that they leave behind. Try your hand at animal tracking with these tips below.

Where to Look

Tracks are most visible when they are left in soft, sticky earth, like mud or wet sand. Prints can also be left behind in the snow. Try looking for tracks after it has snowed or rained—or in places where the ground tends to be wet, such as riverbanks or the beach.

When to Look

Nocturnal animals are active at night, which means their tracks will often be fresh in the morning. Some animals, like squirrels and many birds, are active all day. At the beach, low tide is a good time to spot tracks because that's when birds stop by to hunt for meals.

Draw the tracks you find here.

How to Identify Tracks

Take a look at the size of the track—is it tiny, medium, or big? This will help you narrow down what animal it might belong to right away. Look at the toes of the track as well. Most mammals leave tracks with four or five toe prints. Birds have three forward-facing long toes and one backward-facing toe. Animals like deer have hooves.

What animal (or animals) do you think left the tracks? Draw it here.

Take It Further

Once you are back home, have an adult help you look up more information online about the tracks you found.

Wild about Nuts

Each of these squirrels has a favorite type of nut. Can you solve this maze to figure out which squirrel likes which nut?

Keep an Animal Log

Find a comfortable spot outdoors to observe animals. This can be at a local park, in a backyard, or anywhere animals like to hang out. Try visiting the spot at different times during the day over several days. Use this space to record what you see. Do the same types of animals visit each day? Are there different animals at different times of the day?

Tip!
Too much noise or movement can spook wild animals. Try sitting quietly for a while to let the animals get used to you.

Make a Reptile Rockery

Build a fun place for reptiles to sunbathe with these easy steps!

You Need

- Large collection of big and small rocks and stones
- Quiet, outdoor spot that gets a lot of sun

1. Begin by arranging your larger rocks and stones in a large pile in your sunny spot.

2. Add smaller rocks and stones on top. Arrange them in a way that there are lots of little entrances in and out of the rock pile.

3. Wait. If you've arranged the rockery on grass, allow the grass to grow around it. (This may take several days or weeks.) The grass will give the reptiles places to hide.

4. Watch as small reptiles sun themselves on the rocks!

Cold-Blooded Creatures

Animals that are cold-blooded, like reptiles, cannot naturally maintain their body temperatures the way warm-blooded animals can. When warm-blooded animals, like humans, eat food, the energy from the food creates heat. Since cold-blooded animals can't do this, they keep warm by basking in the sun. To cool off, they find a shady spot to retreat to. As for humans? They sweat!

Safety Tip!
Always observe the rockery from a safe distance. Do not try to touch or catch animals.

Imagine you have turned into a reptile that's lounging in the rockery. How do you like being cold-blooded and having a tail? What new foods do you try? Do you become friends with the other reptiles in the rockery? Write a story about it here.

Hold an Animal Race

In this race, you're the animal! Set up a starting and finish line. Then grab some friends or family members and see who can race from start to finish the fastest. The only catch is, you all have to move like a specific animal. Try these suggestions or come up with your own.

Wolf
Everyone must race on all fours.

Kangaroo
Hop from start to finish.

Horse
Who can gallop the fastest?

Worm
Inch along on your tummy!

Tip!
Don't do anything that makes you uncomfortable, and make sure to race in a place without sharp rocks or sticks.

Wombat Path

Help this burrowing wombat through the twisting tunnels of her den.

Start

Finish

Insect Mania

View insects up close by making a catch-and-release bug jar.

You Need

- Mason jar with lid
- Marker
- Screen from an old splatter screen or sieve, or breathable but strong fabric such as burlap
- Box cutter or scissors
- Low-heat glue gun
- Glue
- Small items from nature such as leaves and twigs

1. Separate the jar's lid from the lid ring. Set the lid aside to use in another craft. Using the lid ring and a marker, trace a circle onto the screen material.

2. Have an adult help you cut out the screen circle.

3. With an adult's help, glue the screen circle to the inside of the lid ring.

4. Fill your jar with a few small items that you find outdoors on the ground, such as leaves and twigs.

5. With an adult's supervision, find an insect that you want to observe. Make sure it is not an insect that can bite, sting, or otherwise harm you. Have an adult help you use the lid to carefully scoop the insect into the jar. Close the lid with the insect inside.

6. Check out the insect! When you are done, make sure to release the insect back where you found it.

Tip!

Whenever possible, scoop the insect into the jar without touching it. Make sure to handle the insect very carefully so as not to harm it.

Use this space to take notes on your insect
and make a detailed drawing of it.

Nighttime Animals

With an adult's permission, find a quiet place outside to sit when it is dark. Can you hear any nocturnal animal noises? Depending on where you live, you might hear owls, bats, insects, coyotes, and more. What do you think the animals you hear are chattering about? Make up a conversation and write it here.

_____

_____

_____

_____

_____

_____

_____

_____

_____

_____

_____

_____

How would your life be different if you were nocturnal? Write a story about it here.

_____

_____

_____

_____

_____

_____

_____

_____

_____

_____

Nocturnal Animals

Nocturnal animals tend to sleep during the day and are active at night. For many animals, this helps them avoid daytime predators. For others, it is an opportunity to hunt fellow nocturnal animals. Being awake at night also means that an animal can escape the heat of the day—which is especially useful for those that live in very hot places, such as deserts.

Animals-About-Town

Solve this maze and collect the right letters as you go to answer the riddle at the bottom of the next page.

E
U
K
Finish
E
A
G
P
J
S
D
A
A
M
C
Y
T
N
T
I
E
Start
F
L

Describe your neighborhood from a local animal's point of view. How might it see things differently? Where are its favorite spots?

_____

_____

_____

_____

_____

_____

_____

_____

_____

_____

_____

What is a bat's favorite game?

___ ___ ___ - ___ ___ ___ - ___ ___ ___ ___

Find a beautiful outdoor view and paint or draw a picture of it.

Quick Challenges
EXPLORE NATURE

Research different kinds of homes that animals make from nature (such as burrows or nests) and draw an amazing animal home here.

Write a poem about your favorite type of weather.

_____

_____

_____

_____

Find a neat-looking flower or plant and draw it here.

_____

_____

_____

_____

Go on a short walk and see how many plants you can name. List them here.

_____

_____

_____

_____

Describe your favorite way to spend a day outdoors.

_____

_____

_____

See the Sights

Design a walking tour of your neighborhood, yard, or local park. Where would you start and end? What things would you point out? What secrets could you reveal? Is there any interesting history? Use this space to write down your ideas.

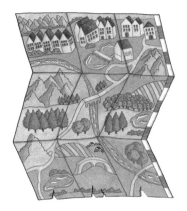

With an adult's supervision, go on your own walking tour.
Then draw a map of your tour here.

Make Leaf Art

Use the beauty of nature to create awesome art.

Tip! Make sure to collect leaves that have already fallen to the ground.

FEEL IT OUT

You Need

- Leaves
- Blank paper
- Crayons or oil pastels

1. On a flat surface, arrange your leaves and cover them with a piece of paper.

2. Hold the paper down with one hand. With your other hand, rub the side of a crayon or pastel over the paper. Impressions of the leaves should start to appear.

PAINT WITH LEAVES

You Need

- Leaves
- Acrylic paints or watercolor paints
- Paintbrush
- Paper, cardstock, or watercolor paper

1. Pick your paint colors.

2. Using the paintbrush or the paint bottles, place dabs of paint onto your chosen leaf in different patterns or arrangements.

3. When you are satisfied, press the leaf onto your paper paint-side down. Remove the leaf.

4. Repeat as many times as you would like.

LEAF IT BEHIND

You Need

- Flat spot outdoors
- Leaves
- Other natural items, such as rocks, moss, and twigs, as well as petals and flowers that have already fallen to the ground

1. Pick a flat spot outdoors.

2. Arrange your materials into different patterns or use them to create images of animals or landscapes.

3. When you are done, leave your art—part of the fun is seeing how long it lasts (or doesn't!).

Plant a Butterfly Garden

Butterflies are beautiful insects. They're also great pollinators. Planting a butterfly garden is a great way to encourage butterflies to visit your yard or even your balcony, roof, or other outdoor space.

You Need

- A good location
- Various flowers, trees, and shrubs that are native to your area
- Large, flat rocks
- Birdbath (optional)
- Soil
- Sand (optional)
- Shovels
- Trowels
- Water
- Pencil and paper

1. Make a plan. A successful butterfly garden begins with making good decisions.

2. Pick the right location. Choose a spot that gets at least six hours of sunlight a day and provides shelter from the wind. If you have a plot in the ground, make sure it's a chemical-free zone. Pesticides are dangerous for butterflies. If you don't have a plot, you can also create a butterfly garden using a collection of containers on a patio.

3. Pick the right plants for butterflies. Adult butterflies drink nectar from flowers. They are attracted to red, yellow, orange, pink, and purple blooms with wide, flat clusters or large, flat petals. Research and choose plants that grow well and are native to where you live.

4. Pick the right plants for caterpillars. Caterpillars eat other plant parts. They are picky eaters. Each species eats specific kinds of plants. Butterflies usually lay eggs on the plants their caterpillars eat. For example, monarch butterflies lay their eggs only on milkweed plants.

5. Draw your idea. Include trees and shrubs for shelter. Add big flat rocks so butterflies have a place to rest. Include a birdbath or spot with wet sand or soil so they have a place to drink water. Clump flowers of the same kind together so butterflies can see them from a distance. What else would your dream butterfly garden include?

6. Review your garden plan with a grown-up. When you're ready, get to work!

Go Stargazing

With an adult's permission, set up a comfy spot outside when it is dark and watch the stars. Do you see any constellations? Draw them here, and then make up a new constellation based on the stars you see.

Super Stargazing

Check out these tips for the best stargazing.
• If you can, find a spot away from bright lights with an unobscured view of the sky.
• Check the weather forecast to make sure you go gazing on a clear night, and wear clothing that will keep you warm.
• Look up what constellations and planets will be visible in your area that night.

What would be your number one wish to make on a shooting star? What would it be like if your wish came true? Write about it here.

_____

_____

_____

_____

_____

_____

_____

_____

_____

_____

_____

_____

_____

Shooting Stars

Though they're called shooting stars, those bright streaks across the night sky are actually meteors. These are relatively small pieces of space rocks. When these rocks enter Earth's atmosphere at superfast speeds, they heat up and eventually burn away, causing

Make an Underwater Viewer

Get a close-up view of a nearby stream or pond with this underwater viewer.

1. Have an adult use the box cutter to completely cut out the bottom of the container.

2. Next, have the adult cut out the center part of the lid, leaving just the frame.

3. Cover the sides of the container in duct tape. This will help block out any light.

4. Stretch a piece of plastic wrap over the top of the container. Close the lid over the plastic wrap. You should now have a see-through window of plastic wrap.

5. To use your viewer, lower the end with plastic wrap into the water. Look through the bottom part of the container, keeping it above the water line. What do you see?

Safety Tip! If your viewer has any sharp edges after it has been cut, have an adult help you cover them with duct tape.

Safety Tip! Ask an adult for help with anything sharp.

Winding Waterways

Find the one path from START to FINISH. Then use the letters along the correct path to spell the name of an endangered Everglades animal.

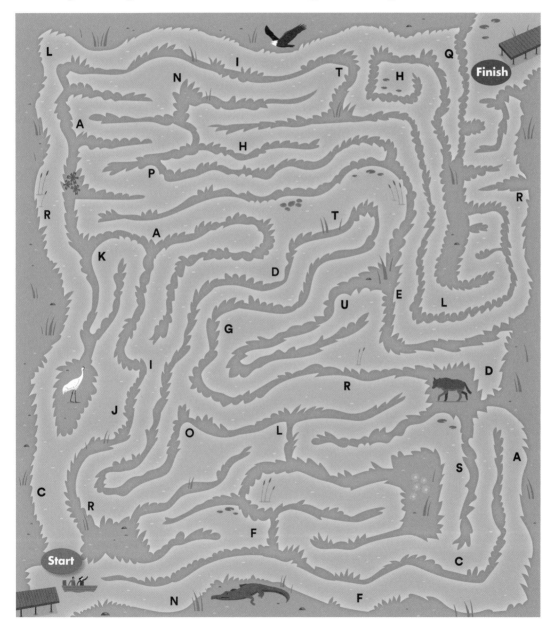

—— —— —— —— —— ——   —— —— —— —— —— ——

Make a Suncatcher

Use bits of nature to craft cool art that catches the sun.

You Need

- Flat natural items such as petals, flowers, and leaves
- Large stick
- Clear contact paper
- 5 mason jar lid rings (pop out the jar lid from each lid ring and set it aside for another craft)
- Marker
- Scissors
- String, twine, or yarn
- Glue (optional)

1. Grab an adult and go on a walk to collect small natural items such as petals, leaves, and flowers, as well as a sturdy, large stick. Make sure to pick up items that have already fallen onto the ground.

2. When you have your materials, lay a piece of contact paper on a flat surface. Using the mason jar lid rings and your marker, trace 10 circles onto the contact paper. Have an adult help you cut out each circle.

3. Peel off the protective backing from five circles and lay each one sticky-side up. In each circle, arrange your natural items however you would like.

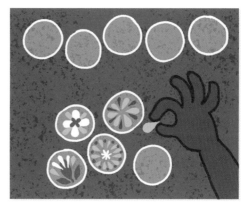

4. When you are satisfied, peel off the backing from the last five circles. Place a second circle sticky-side down over each of the five first ones. Press down so each set of circles sticks together.

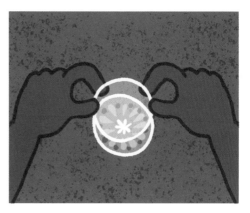

5. Tie a length of string to each lid ring. Then press a circle with your natural items into each lid ring. If you want, you can use glue to secure the circles in place.

6. Tie the other end of each string to the large stick. Make sure each circle hangs at about the same height.

7. Use a piece of string to hang your suncatcher in a window or somewhere sunny outdoors.

Creative Clouds

Head outside on a cloudy day. What shapes do you see in the clouds? Draw some of them here.

Write a story based on three shapes you can find in the clouds.

Outdoor Inspiration

Go to or think about your favorite outdoor spot. Draw it here.

Now write a poem about something you see or feel
when you are in this outdoor space.

_____

_____

_____

_____

_____

_____

_____

_____

_____

_____

_____

_____

_____

_____

Terrific Trees

Can you go from the ground to the top floor without waking any bats?

Bonus! How many birds are in the scene?

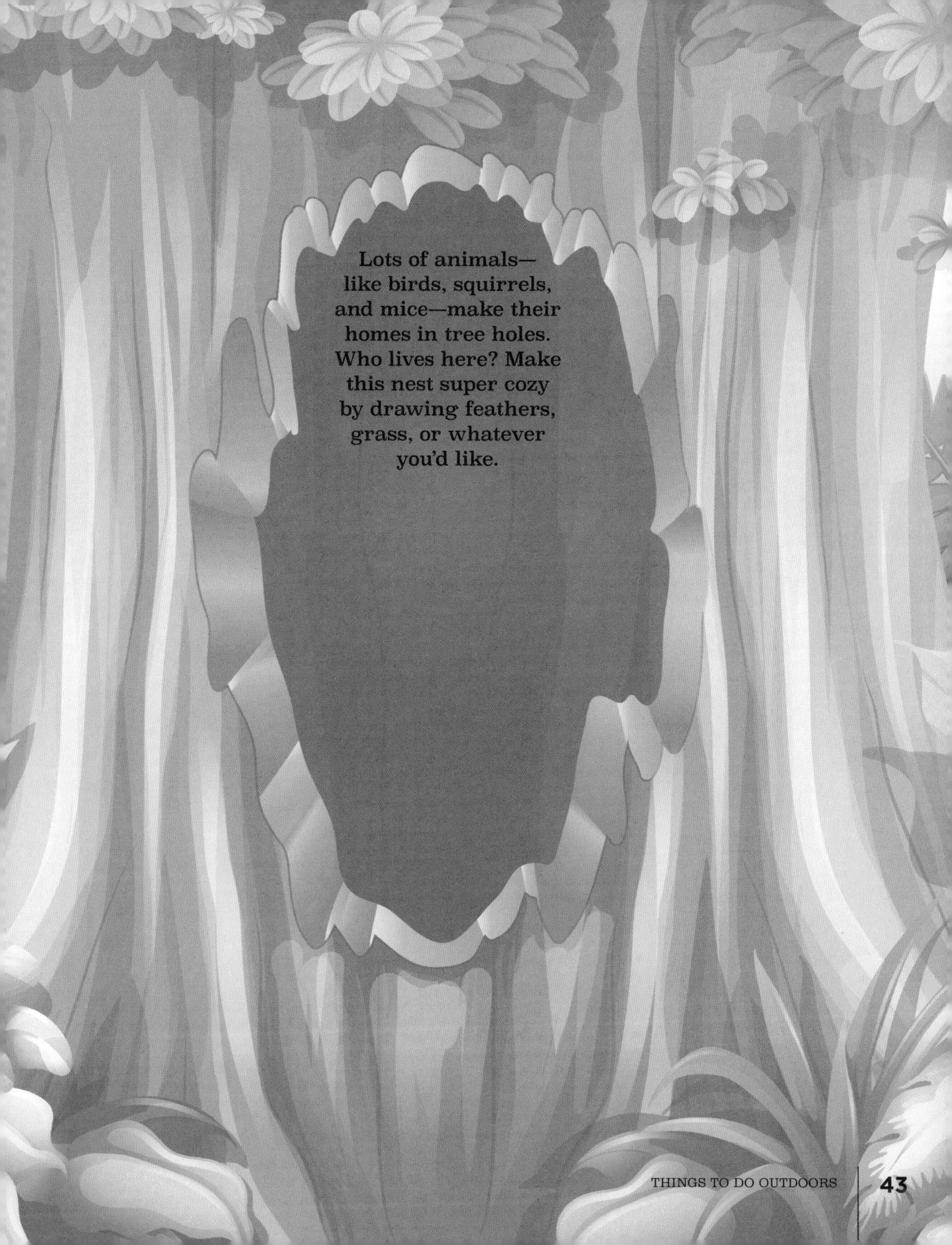

Lots of animals—
like birds, squirrels,
and mice—make their
homes in tree holes.
Who lives here? Make
this nest super cozy
by drawing feathers,
grass, or whatever
you'd like.

What is your favorite messy activity to do outside? Write about it here.

_____

_____

_____

_____

_____

_____

_____

Quick Challenges
GETTING MESSY

Build a structure outside using fallen twigs, leaves, and acorns—then create a mess by knocking the structure down!

Pretend you're planning the messiest picnic of all time. Write a menu for the event that features the messiest meals you can think of.

_____

_____

_____

_____

_____

Write a short story about the messiest animal you can think of.

_____

_____

_____

_____

_____

_____

_____

_____

_____

_____

_____

Challenge a friend to see who can make the biggest splash in a puddle.

Make muddy art! Splatter, paint, or draw with mud on a piece of paper.

Water Games

When it gets too hot, beat the heat with these fun activities!

MAKE SPONGE SOAKERS

You Need

- Clean sponges you can cut up
- Scissors
- Rubber bands

1. Have an adult help you cut each sponge into six to eight equal strips.

2. Bunch the sponge strips together in an asterisk shape (*), and secure them in the middle with rubber bands.

3. Dunk them in cold water and you're ready to go!

WATER BALLOON MUSICAL "CHAIRS"

You Need

- Group of friends or family
- Portable device that can play music
- Sponge soaker

Grab a group of family members or friends. Designate one person to be the music player and have everyone else sit in a circle. When the music player plays a song, those in the circle should pass a wet sponge soaker from one person to another. When the music stops, the person holding the sponge soaker is "out"—and has to squeeze the soaker over their own head!

WATER DODGEBALL

Use the sponge soakers to play a game of dodgeball with friends or family. Make sure to toss the "ball" gently at each other. If you get hit, you're out!

Come up with a water-based game of your own. It could be in a pool, around a sprinkler, or something else entirely. Write the rules here.

Fun with Chalk

MAKE CHALK CHARACTERS

You Need

- Chalk
- Clothes that can get dirty

Take It Further

Try tracing each other while you make silly poses.

Grab a friend or family member and find a large, safe, flat piece of pavement that you can draw on (stay out of any streets or crowded areas). Lie down on the ground on your back.

Have a friend trace all around you with a piece of chalk so that there is a chalk outline of you on the ground. Then trace your friend. Turn the outlines into characters by using more chalk to draw faces, hair, and clothes.

Use this space to write a story about the chalk people you've created. Make sure to include fun mischief for them to get up to!

_____

_____

_____

_____

_____

_____

_____

MAKE CHALK SCENERY

You Need

- Chalk
- Clothes that can get dirty
- Camera
- Friend or family member

1. On a large, safe, flat piece of pavement, draw a funny life-size scene. For example, you could draw an alien sleepover in outer space or a unicorn dance party. Use this space to sketch some ideas.

2. Next, lie down on the ground so that it looks like you are part of the scene! Have your friend or family member stand over you and take a fun picture.

Pond Life

Can you find all the objects in this watery scene?
Once you do, add some color to this busy pond.

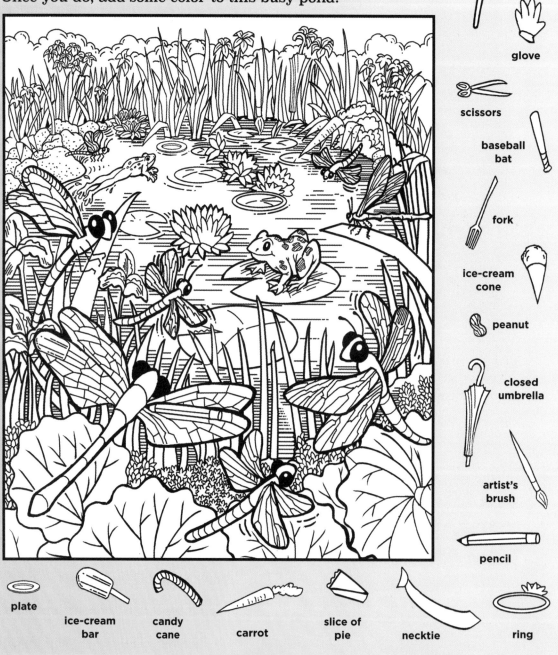

toothbrush

glove

scissors

baseball
bat

fork

ice-cream
cone

peanut

closed
umbrella

artist's
brush

pencil

plate

ice-cream
bar

candy
cane

carrot

slice of
pie

necktie

ring

MAKE A SMALL POND

Create a cool spot to attract local wildlife.

You Need

- Large waterproof container, such as a bucket, storage bin, or plant pot
- Soil
- Stones of different sizes, such as rocks, pebbles, or gravel
- Small logs (optional)
- Bark for shelter (optional)
- Rainwater
- 2 to 3 aquatic plants

Safety Tip!
Don't add animals or water from another body of water to your pond. Instead, wait for creatures to move in!

1. Ask for an adult's permission before doing this activity. If they say yes, find a good spot that gets both shade and sunlight. This is where you will place the pond.

2. Put a layer of soil across the bottom of the container.

3. Start adding some stones inside the container. Try to stack them at different heights and create a way for creatures to get in and out of the pond. Add some stones or small logs next to the outside of the container as well, so animals can climb in and then back out.

4. If you want, add in some curved pieces of bark for shelter.

5. Fill the pond with water. Rainwater works best, as tap water is treated for humans.

6. Plant your plants. Then see which animals come hang out at your pond!

Aquatic Plants

Some good plants to grow in your pond include:
- Yellow flag
- Miniature water lily
- Frogbit
- Starwort
- Flowering rush
- Lesser spearwort

Messy Art

TIE-DYE A BULL'S-EYE

Make a colorful tie-dye design!

You Need

- Tarp or newspapers
- Something white to dye, such as a T-shirt or towel
- Tie-dye kit (found in most craft stores, big box stores, and online)
- Latex gloves (or non-latex gloves if you have an allergy)
- Rubber bands
- Plastic wrap or large plastic bag, such as a trash bag
- Clothes you can get dye on
- Warm water

1. Have an adult help you set up an outdoor work space by laying down a tarp or newspaper. Make sure you wear clothing that you don't mind getting dye on.

2. Wash the item you plan to dye, but don't dry it—leave it damp.

3. Have an adult help you prepare the dye according to the instructions on the kit.

4. When everything is ready, lay your item out flat. To do a bull's-eye pattern, pinch a small bit of fabric at the item's center. Pull this fabric into a large point and secure it with a rubber band.

5. Hold up the top of the point so the rest of the item hangs down. A few inches beneath the first rubber band, add a second.

6. Continue adding rubber bands until you reach the bottom of the item, keeping space between each band.

7. Put on your plastic gloves. Using dye colors of your choice, color each segment of clothing between the rubber bands. Use one color per segment.

8. When you're finished, either wrap the item in plastic wrap or store it securely in a plastic bag. Let the dye soak in for at least six hours, or however long is recommended in the kit instructions.

9. After you've waited, rinse your item with warm water until the water runs clear. Then wash the item in the washing machine. Once it's dry, it's ready!

Take It Further

Try dyeing items in other patterns, too! What happens if you crumple a shirt into a ball and secure it with rubber bands before adding color? Or do items look different if you fold them in interesting ways?

SPRAY PAINTING

Use water blasters or spray bottles to make exciting outdoor art.

You Need

- Watercolor paper
- Easel (optional) or tape
- Water blasters or spray bottles
- Liquid watercolor paints

1. Have an adult help you attach your paper to the easel or tape it against a surface you can get paint on.

2. Fill your water blasters or spray bottles with paint, using a different color for each container.

3. Squirt the paint at the paper!

Come up with some other ways to make unique, messy art. You could mix watercolors with shaving cream, toss paint-filled balloons at a canvas, or think of something brand-new. Use this space to brainstorm, or sketch what art created by this new method would look like.

Muddy Mayhem

Write a story about pigs enjoying the mud. Are they having a spa day or maybe holding a wrestling contest? Come up with the funniest tale you can think of!

Bring your hilarious story to life by drawing some scenes here.

Spend a Rainy Day Outdoors

Why not embrace the rain? Try these marvelously messy ideas or create some of your own.

Race Leaves

Grab a friend and some leaves and see whose leaf boat goes down a stream of water more quickly.

Build a Dam

Find a small stream of running water, and then use twigs and rocks to build a dam. Make sure to dismantle the dam once you're done.

Make Rain Art

Use oil pastels to draw or color on a piece of watercolor paper. Then take your art out into the rain to see how it changes.

Take Photos

Grab a water-proof camera for an artistic photo shoot.

After you're done and dried off, write a poem about your time in the rain.

Make a Mud Masterpiece

CREATE A MUD CASTLE

Follow these instructions to make mud bricks that you can use to build cool creations.

You Need

- Mud
- Small shovel
- Large container or bowl you can get dirty
- Stirring tool, such as a strong stick or a spoon that can get muddy
- Straw or grass (optional)
- Ice cube trays, muffin tins, or small recycled containers that can get dirty
- Clothes that can get dirty

1. Use your shovel to scoop mud into your large container. If it's raining or you live somewhere with lots of mud, you will already have plenty! Otherwise, scoop dirt and soil into the container. Then use the stirrer to mix the dirt and soil with water until it is thick and muddy.

2. If you want, mix in pieces of grass or straw. This will make the bricks stronger.

3. Fill your trays, tins, or small containers with mud.

4. Leave your bricks to dry in the sun for at least two days. When they are ready, pop them out and build a mud structure.

Tip!
Always thoroughly wash your hands after handling dirt or mud.

THE COOLEST CASTLE

Draw the coolest building made of mud that you can think of.

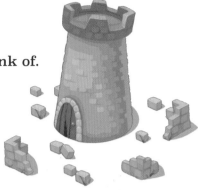

Mud Homes

For thousands of years, people have made bricks and even magnificent buildings out of mud. This was especially useful for people who lived in places without many stones or trees for wood. Mud homes are also easy to keep warm in cold weather and cool in hot weather.

Quick Challenges
OUTDOOR ADVENTURES

With help from an adult, try an outdoor activity you've never done before, like nature photography, skateboarding, or hiking.

What items would you want in an explorer's kit? List them here.

_____

_____

_____

_____

Make an explorer's map of a local outdoor spot, like a beach, park, or hiking trail.

Go rainbow hunting after a storm. If you find a rainbow, draw it here.

Grab an adult and go on a walk through your neighborhood. Create secret nicknames or code names for your favorite places, and list them here.

_____

_____

_____

_____

Make a list of the top three outdoor adventures you would like to try.

_____

_____

_____

_____

Put on a Nighttime Shadow Show

Tip!
Practice setting up and performing your shadow show before debuting it for your audience.

Have a nighttime adventure by putting on a show in the dark—using shadows!

You Need

- Large white sheet that you can bring outside
- Rope, string, or twine
- Clothespins
- Flashlights
- Props (optional)

1. First, plot out your show. Who will come to watch it? Who will be performing—you alone or you and others? Decide whether it will be a play, dance, or a skit, and what you'll use to make your shadows. Brainstorm some ideas here.

2. Next, set up your stage. Have an adult help you hang your white sheet outdoors by stringing up the rope and securing the sheet to it with clothespins. Make sure that the sheet is big enough to cover whatever you will be using to cast shadows, and that there is room both in front of and behind it.

3. When it gets completely dark, your performance can begin! Have your audience sit in front of the sheet and your actors behind it. When you're ready, shine the flashlights from behind the sheet so the light hits the sheet's back side. (You can have someone hold the flashlights or prop them up so they aim toward the sheet.) Now, when you move between the flashlights and the sheet, your audience will be able to see a shadow.

Have a friend or family member hold a flashlight and cast a shadow on this page. It can be a shadow of their hand, an action figure, or whatever they think of. Trace it here and then turn it into a cool drawing.

Make a Fort

Create a cool cardboard palace or secret hideaway with these easy-to-make forts.

CARDBOARD PALACE

You Need

- Recycled cardboard boxes or other large pieces of cardboard
- Duct tape
- Tarp (optional)
- Paint (optional)
- Scissors (optional)

1. Gather as many recycled cardboard boxes and pieces of cardboard as you can. The more you have, the bigger your fort will be (though a tiny fort can be fun, too!).

2. Use the space below to sketch out how these boxes and pieces can be transformed into a fort. You can use scissors to cut out doors or windows, stack boxes on top of each other, connect pieces to form tunnels, or use different boxes as different rooms.

3. If you want, lay down a tarp first to keep your fort dry. When you're ready, use the duct tape to secure your fort together. You can even decorate the outside with paint.

DRAW YOUR FORT HERE!

Tip!
Make sure to gather sticks that are already on the ground.

SECRET STICK LEAN-TO

You Need

- Long sticks and twigs all about the same height (try to find ones at least 3 feet long)
- Flat surface to lean your fort against, such as a fence or wall
- Twine or string (optional)
- Fallen leaves (optional)

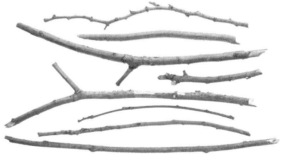

1. After you have gathered enough sticks, find a flat spot of earth near a wall, fence, or other surface.

2. Begin leaning the sticks against the wall so they form a triangle large enough for you to fit inside. The more sticks you add, the more hidden you will be under them.

3. If you want, secure the sticks with twine, or add fallen leaves to the outside to camouflage it.

Give your fort a name and write some fort rules here.

Write a journal entry while inside your fort.

Cave Quest

Bonus! Can you also find the ice pop, adhesive bandage, ice-cream cone, and sock?

In this big picture, find the envelope, yo-yo, artist's brush, pencil, ruler, bowling pin, snake, carrot, teacup, glove, comb, potato, button, frying pan, tack, crescent moon, and slice of pizza.

frying pan

artist's brush

envelope

yo-yo

ruler

bowling pin

snake

carrot

pencil

tack

crescent moon

button   potato   teacup   glove   comb   slice of pizza

If there was a secret city or an underground cavern hidden near your home, what do you think it would be like? Imagine that you are an explorer who has discovered this incredible site and write a story about it here.

Nature Scavenger Hunt

The outdoors are full of incredible things—how many can you spot? See if you can find every item on this list.

To Find

- ☐ A blue feather
- ☐ A perfectly round stone
- ☐ A colorful sunset or sunrise
- ☐ Five different insects
- ☐ Two snails or slugs
- ☐ An enormous leaf
- ☐ A purple flower
- ☐ A wild fruit, vegetable, or nut
- ☐ A tree covered in vines
- ☐ A bird's nest

Make your own scavenger hunt for a friend or family member by listing some of your favorite things to find in nature here, and then see if you can spot them together.

_____

_____

_____

_____

_____

_____

_____

_____

_____

_____

_____

Safety Tip!
• Don't explore alone. Take an adult or friend with you.
• Remember to look but never touch.
• If you are not sure if an animal is poisonous or dangerous, move away from it.
• Take a reusable water bottle with you.
• Stay on marked paths and trails.

Host a Game Day

Plan a just-for-fun athletic adventure for friends or family. Try these fun activities here or come up with some of your own.

CREATE AN OBSTACLE COURSE

Set up your obstacle course in a safe area. The person who completes it the fastest wins! Here are some obstacle course ideas to get you started:

• Make a tunnel of hoops, pool noodles, or cardboard boxes.
• Have participants weave around buckets or planters.
• Limbo under a piece of string you tie up.
• Lay a rope on the ground. Walk across it as if balancing on a tightrope.

Disc Throw

See who can fling a flying disc the farthest.

Take a Tumble

See who can do the most somersaults, or have participants invent new ways to tumble.

Can Throw

Set up a pyramid of recycled tin cans. See who can knock it down from the farthest distance.

What other fun—or funny—competitions can you think of? Come up with some here.

OPENING CEREMONY

Lots of amazing athletic competitions have opening performances that introduce the players and entertain the crowd. Whether it is a song, dance, parade, or something else, come up with a grand opening ceremony for your Game Day. Brainstorm it here.

AWESOME AWARDS

Come up with different awards to give out to all your participants. Sketch the award ribbons here, and then draw them on another piece of paper and cut them out.

Picnic Fun

Look at the grids. Each numbered square tells you how many of the empty squares touching it (above, below, left, right, or diagonally) contain an ant. Write an **X** on squares that can't have an ant. Then write an **A** on squares that have an ant.

Hints!

- Put an X on all the squares touching a zero.
- Look in the corners where a numbered square may make it more obvious where an ant is hiding.
- An ant cannot go in a square that has a number.

This grid has 4 ants.

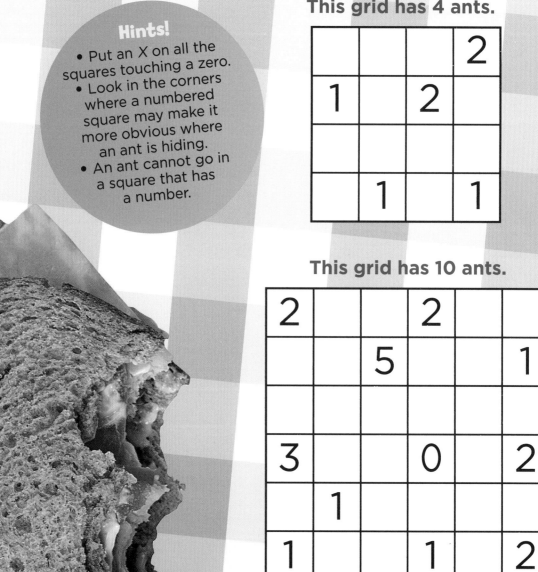

			2
1		2	
	1		1

This grid has 10 ants.

2		2			
	5				1
3			0		2
	1				
1			1		2

PLAN A PICNIC HIKE

With an adult's help, plan a short hike (or walk) and bring a picnic to enjoy at the end. You can choose to walk a local hiking trail or stroll through a part of the park you've never been to—or even wander through new parts of your neighborhood. Finish off your adventure with a feast.

Where will you hike? Plan your route here.

_____

_____

_____

_____

_____

_____

_____

What picnic foods will you bring?

_____

_____

_____

_____

Tip!
Have an adult help you pick the best shoes for your hike and pack your supplies.

Tip!
Bring foods that are easy to carry and to eat with your hands.

Nature by Night

With an adult, take a nighttime walk through an area you normally go to during the day. This could be through a park, around your block, or by the beach. How is it different from when it's light out? Write your observations here.

_____

_____

_____

_____

_____

_____

_____

_____

_____

_____

_____

_____

_____

_____

Draw a picture inspired by your night walk here.

Keep track of time for a day using just the position of the sun in the sky.

Quick Challenges
SUPER SCIENCE

Grab a magnifying glass and inspect some plants up close. Draw what you see here.

Draw or photograph the moon as it changes over the course of one month.

Place a glass filled with water in a sunny spot. Move the glass around to see if you can make your own rainbow (and drink the water when you're done!).

What is a science question you have about the great outdoors? Write it here, and then grab an adult and see if you can find the answer online or in a book.

Design a vehicle that can explore the deep sea.

Digging Dinosaurs

With an adult's help, look up what kinds of dinosaurs lived closest to your area millions of years ago. Using the information you find, write a story about going on an archaeological dig in your region. What materials would you bring on the dig? What kinds of dinosaurs would you find?

Imagine that you discovered a never-before-seen dinosaur on your dig.
Draw it here.

Design a Raft

Create a miniature raft that really floats.

You Need

- Small sticks of about the same size or craft sticks
- Low-heat glue gun
- Glue
- Scrap paper (optional)

Have an adult help you glue your sticks together side by side to form a flat square shape. If you want, add a mast and paper flag. Test out your raft in a nearby stream, river, pond, or fountain. Does it float? Write your observations here.

_____

_____

_____

_____

_____

_____

_____

_____

_____

_____

_____

_____

_____

Based on what you observed with your first raft, come up with some cool new designs that you think will float. How tall can you make your next raft? How big? Can you add multiple stories? Draft some designs here, and then build them and test them out.

Rainy Day

To go from this maze's rainy START to its sunny FINISH, you have to find the path that takes you through alternating clouds and sun. Your path cannot cross itself or go through two of the same symbols in a row.

Find a place outdoors that looks beautiful or amazing to you. It can be in a friend's backyard, at the beach, or anywhere you like. Draw this place in four different types of weather. What changes or stays the same?

Sun Prints

Safety Tip!
Don't forget to wear sunscreen!

Shadows usually disappear when the sun goes down—but they won't in this experiment! Use the sun's rays to make shadow art!

You Need

- Items that can be pressed flat, like leaves
- Bright-colored construction paper
- Plastic wrap
- 4 different-sized rocks

1. Collect leaves and other items for your sun print.

2. Place the construction paper outside on a flat surface.

3. Arrange your leaves and other objects on the construction paper to create a design.

4. Place a piece of plastic wrap on top of your sun print. Smooth the plastic out as best as you can.

5. Place a rock on each corner to hold the plastic wrap in place.

6. Leave the print in the sun for 3 to 4 hours.

7. Remove the leaves and other items and observe your artwork.

The Scoop on Sun Prints

Sunlight is made of lots of different kinds of light mixed together. One of these kinds of light is called *ultraviolet (UV) light*. UV light can break apart some of the chemicals that make color in construction paper and cause it to fade. It can't get through the leaves and other objects, though, so these leave a bright-colored "shadow" on the paper.

Create a drawing inspired by your sun prints here.

Volcano Science

Can you find all the explosive words in this list?

Word List

ACTIVE
ASH
BASALT
BLAST
CINDER CONE

CRATER
DORMANT
ERUPT
FISSURE
HOT SPOT

LANDSLIDE
LAVA
MAGMA
MOLTEN ROCK
MOUNTAIN

PUMICE
SPATTER
TREMOR
VENT

```
        Q B T S
        L S N T
    R A A A O S
    I L E R V E N T
    B A B A S A L T
  C I N D E R C O N E
  P A D E A O T R T T
  H U L S E M M I N A B M
  O M F L H G E V F T T Y
  J T I M I N A R E H Y K E X
    P S C P D S M T P U R E U R
  X N P E A E B S M O U N T A I N
  G D O R M A N T U R E T T A P S
  T A T M O L T E N R O C K Y H U
  D M T R A I N I E R S E A T T L E S
```

Bonus Puzzle

Hidden somewhere in the grid is the name of the active volcano pictured on this page and the U.S. city it's near. Look across, down, and diagonally. The words will fit in the spaces below.

__ __. __ __ __ __ __ __ __ , __ __ __ __ __ __ __

ERUPTION!

See an erupting "volcano" up close with this fun science experiment.

You Need

- Recycled plastic bottle
- Sand or mud
- Leaves, moss, toy dinosaurs, or other things to decorate your volcano (optional)
- 3 to 4 teaspoons baking soda
- Funnel
- Dish soap (optional)
- Red or orange food coloring (optional)
- Bottle of white vinegar

1. To build your volcano, stand the plastic bottle upright. Pile sand or mud up around it in a cone shape, leaving the mouth of the bottle open and uncovered.

2. If you want, you can decorate the outside of your volcano with leaves, toys, or anything else.

3. Using the funnel, add the baking soda to the bottle.

4. If you want to make your "lava" bubbly or colorful, add a few drops of dish soap or food coloring—or both.

5. When you are ready for the volcano to erupt, pour in some white vinegar and see what happens!

Behind the Eruption

When vinegar and baking soda interact, they create a gas called *carbon dioxide*. This gas pushes everything up and out of the bottle, like an explosion.

Make Papier-Mâché Bowls

Create paper bowls using newspaper and a "glue" you make yourself.

1. Set up a work space outdoors—this activity is messy!

2. Take your small bowl and turn it upside down. Cover the bottom of it with plastic wrap.

3. Cut the newspaper into equal-sized strips. These should be about one inch thick and long enough to drape over the back of your small bowl from one side to the other.

4. In your mixing container, combine equal parts water and flour and mix them together. Try starting with one cup of each and adding more if you need it.

5. Dip a strip of newspaper into the mixture. Slide your fingers down the strip to remove any extra mixture, and then lay the strip across the bottom of the bowl.

6. Repeat step 5 with another strip, laying it so that it intersects with the first strip. Continue repeating this step, crisscrossing the strips until the bowl is completely covered by newspaper.

7. Use a paintbrush to coat the newspaper-covered bowl with another layer of the flour and water mixture.

8. If you want, add another layer of newspaper strips to the bowl. The more layers you add, the thicker and sturdier the bowl will be.

9. When you are finished, let the bowl dry overnight. Once it is dry, gently remove the small bowl from your papier-mâché bowl by pulling on the plastic wrap.

10. Using the acrylic paints, decorate your bowl however you want. Make sure to let it dry completely between coats.

Gooey Glue

The secret behind papier-mâché lies in *molecules*. Molecules are the small building blocks that make up substances—including water and flour, the substances used to make papier-mâché. Water molecules tend to easily "stick" with other molecules. When water is added to flour, the molecules in the mixture stick to themselves—and to other things. "Sticky" molecules are what make other glues work, too.

Design an Outdoor Invention

Come up with a brand-new invention meant to be used outdoors. First, list some outdoor inventions that already exist—for example, windmills or binoculars.

_____

_____

_____

_____

_____

_____

Is there a way to improve on one of these inventions? Or is there something else that you'd like to see that doesn't exist yet—like a machine that captures lightning or a hat that could keep away mosquitoes? Write about what you come up with here.

_____

_____

_____

_____

Design and draw your brand-new invention!

Parachute Challenge

Make a parachute out of household materials to help guide a weight safely to the ground.

You Need

- Plastic bag or lightweight fabric
- Scissors
- Hole punch
- 8 pieces of string or yarn
- Tape
- Small object with a hole or loop for weight

1. Use the scissors to cut a square from your plastic bag or fabric.

2. Cut off the four corners of the square to make an octagon.

3. Use the hole punch to make a hole in the middle of each side for a total of eight holes.

4. Thread one piece of string through a hole. Gently tie and tape it in place. Repeat for the other holes.

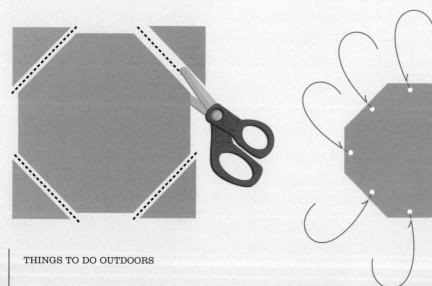

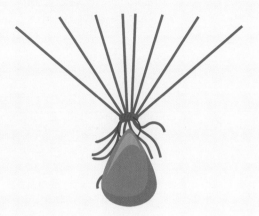

6. Test your parachute: Drop the parachute while standing on a sturdy stool or chair. (Have someone hold the stool or chair while you're standing on it.) Did your weight land gently? If not, try again!

5. Tie the other ends of each string to the weight.

Tip!
Try to make a parachute for a lighter weight . . . and a heavier one! Find out what happens when you punch a small hole in the middle of the parachute.

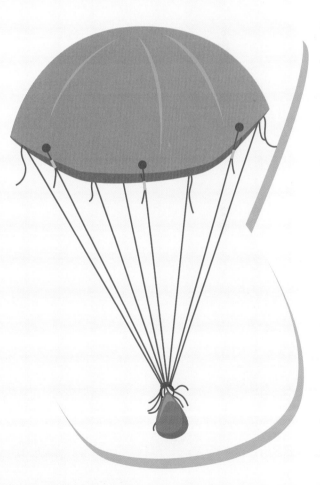

Camouflage Expert

Learn about animal camouflage while practicing your observation skills. First, have an adult help you look up what kinds of animals live near you. Next, find a comfortable spot to sit outdoors. How do you think the different animals stay hidden in this area? Consider whether an animal's size, coat color, and pattern might help it blend in. Write your thoughts down here.

Take It Further

After you've thought about it, research the actual ways these different animals conceal themselves. Were you right, or did the answer surprise you?

Come up with a brand-new species of animal that can perfectly camouflage in this outdoor spot. What does it look like, and where does it hide? How is it so good at camouflage? Draw it here and label the parts that keep the animal hidden.

Paint a rock with a smiley face and leave it where someone might find it.

With an adult's supervision, walk around your block and pick up any trash you see. (Make sure to bring a trash bag and wear protective gloves. Don't touch anything sharp.)

For items you may use often—such as sunscreen, straws, or laundry detergent—try switching to eco-friendly options that are safe for the environment.

Plant a tree.

List three things you can do to help decrease pollution.

_____

_____

_____

_____

_____

_____

Talking to plants can help them grow—write a poem to a plant here, and then read it aloud.

_____

_____

_____

_____

_____

_____

Create Compost

Observe the process of composting with this activity.

You Need

- 2-liter plastic bottle
- Scissors
- Soil
- Old newspapers
- Food scraps (fruit and vegetables, teabags, coffee grounds, etc.)
- Dry leaves and grass clippings
- Spray bottle of water
- Duct tape
- Coffee can lid or plate

1. With help from an adult, cut the top third off the plastic bottle and poke small holes in the bottom and sides of the bottle.

2. Add a layer of soil to the bottom of the bottle. Then add a layer of newspaper. Next, add a layer of food scraps. Finally, add a layer of dead leaves and grass clippings. Spray with water.

3. Repeat step 2 until the bottle is filled. Do not pack the contents down as you add layers.

4. Place the top back on the bottle. Use duct tape to tape it closed.

5. Place the coffee can lid or plate under the bottle. Shake the bottle to mix the ingredients every few days. In two to three months, you will have beautiful soil!

Tip!
This activity lets you see composting in action. But it won't let you compost much of the plant waste you produce. If you'd like to compost on a larger scale, work with an adult to research a composting plan that works for your family.

Composts are sometimes called "worm castles" because worms can help turn rotting materials into soil. Use this space to design what you think a real castle for worms should look like.

Hold an Outdoor Book Sale for Charity

Set up a used book sale, and then donate the proceeds to charity.

With an adult's permission, plan a get-together where you and friends or family members collect gently used books you no longer read. Once you have collected the books you no longer read and want to sell, set up a fundraiser where you sell the books at a discounted price, and donate the funds to a local charity. You can start planning your fundraiser by answering the questions below.

When and where will you hold the event? You could hold it in a driveway, at a local park, or somewhere else with lots of space.

_____

_____

_____

_____

What charity or organization will you donate to? Research some local animal shelters, food banks, environmental groups, or other organizations that work for causes you care about.

_____

_____

_____

_____

What will you charge? You could charge a small fee or ask for donations in return for the books. For example, if you are donating to an animal shelter, people could bring canned dog food or new dog toys.

_____

_____

_____

_____

_____

_____

Are there other types of fundraisers you could hold in the future?
For instance, you could sell lemonade or friendship bracelets for charity.

_____

_____

_____

_____

_____

CREATE A FLYER

Draft a flyer here to help you get the word out about your event. Make sure to include the time and place, as well as the organization you will be supporting.

DECK IT OUT

Use this space to design some decorations and signs for your event.
Then craft them out of construction paper or cardstock.

Removing Invasive Species

Invasive species are species that are not native to an area and cause harm to the new place where they live. These species may be introduced when organisms are carried on ships that travel between different places or when people accidentally release species into new areas. Once there, the organisms can destroy local crops or threaten native animals. Luckily, there are many groups devoted to preventing and clearing out invasive species across the country. See if you and your family can spend a day volunteering with one of these organizations and make a big difference in your own neighborhood!

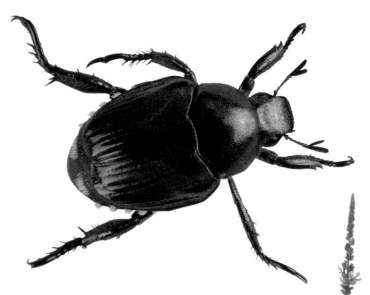

Look up an invasive plant species in your area. On the next page, design a "Wanted" poster for it. Make sure to include an image and description of the plant, what people should do if they find it, and where to go for more resources.

Volunteer Opportunities

Check with your local government to find volunteer groups in your area that work on invasive species prevention and removal.

Nurturing Nature

In addition to being kind to others, it's important to be kind to yourself! Spending time in nature can be good for both your mental and physical health. It can lower stress, decrease anxiety, boost your mood, and even give you more energy. Spend 20 to 30 minutes outside, and then write about how you feel here. Do you feel differently than you did before going outdoors?

SEED SURPRISES

Help spread the joy of nature by making and scattering seed surprises.

You Need

- 3 to 4 packages of wildflower seeds native to your area
- Peat-free potting soil or compost
- Air-dry clay or clay powder (available in craft shops)
- Mixing bowl
- Water
- Baking tray

1. Mix the seeds, potting soil or compost, and clay together in your mixing bowl.

2. Slowly add water until the mixture is wet enough to form into balls. Roll the mixture into as many table tennis–sized balls as you can make.

3. Place your seed surprises on a baking tray and leave to dry for at least three hours.

4. Give your seed surprises to friends and family members to toss in their yards and gardens.

Host a Cleanup

If you spot a local park, beach, or trail that has a problem with trash or litter, why not organize a cleanup group to help take care of it? Follow these steps to get started.

1. **Get Permission:** First, make sure to get permission and supervision from an adult. They may also have some great ideas to add. Next, check whether you need to get permission from your local council or city government. Write down what you find out here.

_____

_____

_____

_____

_____

2. **Do Research:** Find out what you will need to dispose of any trash or recyclable materials you collect. Have an adult help you look up local trash and recycling centers.

_____

_____

_____

_____

_____

Tip!
You can also look for and join in on local cleanups run by others in your area.

3. Pick your location and date.

Tip!
Make sure to bring enough water and wear sunscreen, protective clothing, and sturdy shoes. You may also want to bring a travel firstaid kit.

_____

_____

_____

_____

4. Find a Crew: Decide how big you want your cleanup crew to be. Will it be just family and friends, or do you want to invite your local community? If it's the latter, plan how to get the word out—you can ask an adult to post the event on local online community groups, create flyers, or see if you can add the event to a local newsletter.

_____

_____

_____

_____

Park Cleanup 3:00 p.m.

5. Collect Your Supplies: You may need gloves, trash bags, buckets, trash pickers or grabbers, and clothes you can get dirty. List your supplies here.

_____

_____

_____

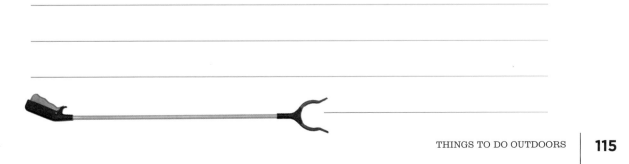

Neighborhood Help

Can you find all the items that don't belong in this garden?

pennant

belt

drinking straw

slipper

teacup

t-shirt

necktie

mailbox

hockey stick

magic wand

ruler

present

magnet

party hat

There are lots of small ways you can help your neighbors and family. Try some of the suggestions below. Then add your own list of ideas here and try them out.

- Rake leaves
- Mow a lawn
- Water plants
- Help out in a garden
- Pull weeds
- Walk a dog

Start a Community Garden

A lot of planning takes place before any plants go in the ground in a community garden.

1. Ask one or more adults to help you with this project. Then find out what kind of garden your community wants: With an adult's help, create a survey about the garden and send it out to people in your community. Collect feedback. Hold a meeting to discuss the results and start making important decisions.

2. Based on the feedback you receive, decide which kind of community garden you want to have. Will everyone have their own plot? Will everyone work as a team on one large garden? Will you keep, sell, or donate the food you grow?

3. Consider finding a sponsor. If you're starting from scratch, a sponsor, like a local business, can help pay for the supplies and tools you'll need to create your garden. With the help of a grown-up, call or email potential sponsors to let them know about your project. Ask if they would be interested in partnering with you.

4. Have an adult help you choose a site. Gardens need healthy soil, at least six hours of sunshine a day, and a dependable water source. Get permission and any necessary permits from your community leaders to create the garden in your selected site.

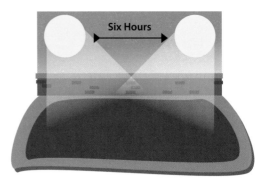

5. Establish the rules. Create a work schedule. Identify work hours and days. Determine, in detail, how you will assign plots, manage weeds and pests, store and share tools, etc. Decide whether you will charge dues. Things will run much more smoothly if everyone agrees on the ground rules from the beginning.

6. Make a plan. Measure the site and draw your plan. Include the length and width of each plant bed. Don't forget to include space for aisles so people can walk between the beds in the garden. You might also want build a fence around your garden to protect it.

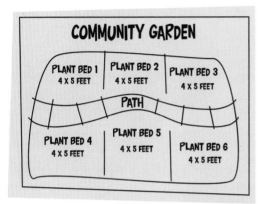

7. Plant the garden. Plan a community workday to clear the land, prepare the soil, and get the plants in the ground.

Tip!
Make a sign that welcomes gardeners but that also tells the story of why your community came together to create the garden. You could also list the garden's rules at the entrance. These signs tell newcomers and visitors how special your space is.

Describe an object you see outside without saying its name and have a friend guess what it is.

Draw a giant tic-tac-toe game in the dirt with a stick or on the pavement with chalk.

Make up the rules to an outdoor sport that aliens might play on Mars and write them here.

_____

_____

_____

_____

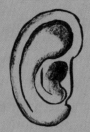 Find a space outside and whistle as loud as you can. From how far away can a friend or family member hear your whistle?

Play an outdoor game of hide-and-seek.

Doodle one of your favorite fun outdoor memories here.

Nighttime Games

Make a glow-in-the-dark bowling set that can be played outdoors in the dark.

- 10 glow sticks
- 10 large recycled water bottles
- Medium-sized ball, such as a soccer ball or rubber ball

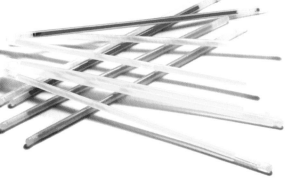

1. Crack each glow stick according to the instructions on the packets, and put one in each water bottle. Close the caps on the bottles afterward.

2. On a flat surface, set up your "pins." Place one bottle in the first row, two in the second, three in the third, and four in the fourth to form a triangle.

3. Move about 20 paces away and roll the ball toward the pins. Try to knock down as many as you can.

4. Take turns bowling with friends or family members!

Consider what other games can be played
in the dark when glow sticks are involved.
Come up with a new game involving
glow sticks and describe it here.

Terrific Tag

There are so many ways to play tag—try one of these suggestions or come up with your own. For each game, you need at least three players.

Footprint Tag

Try playing this game on a sandy beach or in winter after a snowfall, when footprints show up well. Have each player run around the game area once to make footprints. After that, everyone can only step in footprints that have already been made—including whoever is "It."

Flashlight Tag

This version is best played once the sun has set. Give whoever is "It" a flashlight. The other players must try to hide or run from the beam—if the light shines on them, they're "It"!

"It" Frenzy

In this game, everyone is "It"! Players must try to tag each other as many times as they can. Keep count— whoever has tagged the most people at the end is the winner.

Leap Frog Tag

When whoever is "It" tags another player, that player must go to an "out" zone. However, tagged players can be "freed" if they squat down low and another player jumps over their back with legs wide, just like a frog!

Create a Giant Board Game

Come up with a brand-new board game. Then, using chalk, design a giant outdoor version and play it with your friends or family—only, in this game, you act as the game pieces! Use this space here to design how your board looks.

Write down the rules to your game here.

Jump Rope Fun

This game of jump rope has gotten a little out of hand! Help the biker navigate the jump rope maze to join his friends in their game.

Start

Finish

Grab an adult and a jump rope and get hopping with these jumping styles and games.

SOLO JUMPING

You Need

- One-person jump rope

If you're jumping rope on your own, try these different jumping styles—or make up your own:
- Jump on one foot, switching feet each jump.
- Jump rope with your eyes closed.
- Jump in an X pattern: cross your legs on one jump, uncross for the next, and so on.

SPLASH JUMP ROPE

You Need

- Long jump rope
- At least 3 people
- Clear plastic cups
- Water

If you have a small group, have one group member hold one end of the jump rope. Tie the other end to a fence or wall. (If you have enough people, two people can hold and turn the rope.) Each jumper should hold a clear plastic cup full of water and take a turn, jumping and holding the cup for three jumps before jumping out. Whoever has the least amount of water left in their cup is out. Continue and increase the number of jumps each time until you have a winner.

RUSH THE ROPE

You Need

- Long jump rope
- At least 4 people

If you have a small group, have one group member serve as the rope turner and hold one end of the jump rope. Tie the other end to a fence or wall. (If you have enough people, two people can hold and turn the rope.) Have your jumpers form a line. The first person must run under the rope without letting it touch them. Next, two people must run under the rope together. Add a person each time—if the rope touches anyone, you must start from the beginning. See how many people you can get up to.

Chalk Games

Grab some chalk and a few friends or family members for some simple outdoor fun.

THE GROUND IS LAVA

Find a large piece of pavement you can draw on. Using red and orange chalk, assign an area to be lava. Then use black and gray chalk to draw some "stones" through the area. See if you can hop from one stone to another to make it through the course without getting "burned."

GUESS THAT PICTURE!

You Need

- Scrap paper, cut into strips
- Pen or pencil
- Bowl
- At least 4 players
- Stopwatch or timer
- Chalk
- Blank paper (for the artist to draw on)

Have each person write down several objects, animals, people, or places, each on a different strip of paper. Fold each paper strip and mix them all up in the bowl. Form two or more teams, where one person is the artist and the other people on the team are the guessers. During each team's turn, the artist pulls a strip of paper out of the bowl but doesn't show it to anyone else. Next, a timer is set for 30 seconds. The artist should then use chalk to draw the subject they selected onto the pavement. The other team members must try to guess what the object is before the time runs out!

Draw the most extreme hopscotch course you can think of here. If you want, recreate it outside and try it out!

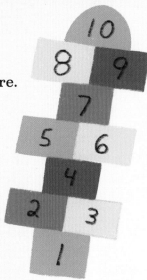

Learn a New Skill

Is there a new skill you've always wanted to learn? Whether it's riding a skateboard or a bike, learning to cartwheel or do a handstand, or mastering the art of hooping, the outdoors are the perfect practicing grounds. Grab an adult and together walk through the following steps.

1. Think about what skill you'd like to learn. Are you interested in fishing? Or would you rather hone your soccer skills? Figure out what interests you the most, and set a specific goal for yourself here.

2. Do your research—grab an adult and head online or to a library. Watching video tutorials from the experts can be a great way to get pointers on a new activity. If you know someone who can help teach you, even better! Write down some steps you've discovered here.

3. Pick the perfect place to practice. If you're learning to cartwheel, think about finding a place with soft grass or using a tumbling mat. If you're learning a specific sport, consider whether there is a public field in your area.

_____

_____

_____

_____

_____

_____

4. Practice a whole lot! Record your results over five different days—or weeks—here.

_____

_____

_____

_____

_____

_____

_____

Host a Parade

What could be more fun than a parade? You don't need to wait for one to come to town—make your own with these simple steps.

1. Think of a theme or reason to celebrate. Perhaps you are throwing a parade in honor of someone you care about or maybe you're celebrating a birthday. Brainstorm your parade theme here.

2. Decide who is participating in the parade. Will friends and family be joining in? Or maybe your marchers are all stuffed animals. Make a list here.

3. Assign roles to each participant. People in parades often play instruments, dance, twirl batons, and more.

☐ _____

☐ _____

☐ _____

☐ _____

☐ _____

☐ _____

4. Pick out some fun music and come up with creative costumes. Sketch your costumes here.

5. When you're ready, assemble your audience and let the parade begin!

Fishy Fun

Can you find the octopus hiding among the fish?
Then find the 12 hidden seashells.

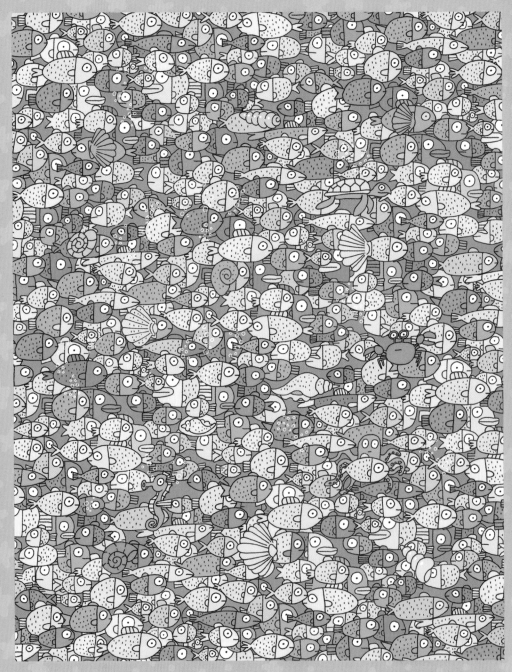

PLAY SARDINES

Join in on the fishy fun with this variation on hide-and-seek.

You Need

- At least 4 people
- Outdoor area with places to hide

1. Select one player who is "It." Only, instead of being the person counting, this player will go off to choose a hiding spot.

2. Have the rest of the group close their eyes and count to 30. During this time, the player who is "It" hides.

3. After counting, the rest of the group should split up to search for the hidden player. However, if a searching player finds the person who's "It," they don't alert the others—instead, they join the hidden player in the hiding spot.

4. As each new searcher discovers the hiding spot, they also crowd in and join the others until the players are packed like sardines! The game is over once the last player has found everyone.

5. The first person to have discovered the hiding player is now "It."

Design a boat made completely from reused items. Draw it here.

Quick Challenges REUSE IT!

Plan the menu for a family cookout using leftovers only. Write it here.

_____

_____

_____

_____

_____

_____

Bring a reusable water bottle when playing outdoors.

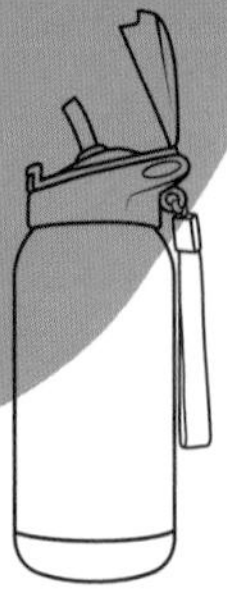

With an adult, visit your local playground and examine the structures. Could you make your own playground—but only out of reused items like tires or plastic bottles? Draw your design here.

List three ways that you reuse items to help the environment.

How might plants and animals recycle in nature? Observe wildlife to get some ideas. Then grab an adult and go online to find out more about nature's recyclers.

Make a Kite

Make a kite that really flies by repurposing a plastic bag.

You Need

- 1 stick or bamboo skewer about 14 inches long
- 1 stick or bamboo skewer about 8 inches long
- String or twine
- Large, repurposed plastic trash bag
- Scissors
- Tape
- Ruler
- Scraps of ribbons, yarn, or string

1. Cross the two sticks so that the shorter stick crosses over the longer one in the shape of a lowercase *t*. Have an adult help you use string to tie the sticks in place.

2. Using four pieces of string, create a diamond-shaped frame around the t-shape. To do this, tie a piece of string from one stick end to the next. Repeat three more times until there are strings running between all four stick ends.

3. Cut any plastic handles off your bag and cut along the two sides of the bag. Unfold the bag and lay it flat so it becomes one long sheet.

4. Lay your kite frame over the flat plastic bag so that the frame fits completely within the plastic. Wrap the sides of the plastic bag around the frame and tape them in place so you now have a large, plastic-covered diamond.

6. Cut a piece of string that is at least six feet long. Tie one end to the middle of the string attached to the short stick. The other end of the long string is the part you hold.

7. If you want, attach ribbons to the bottom of the kite as a tail.

5. Measure a piece of string about 12 inches long. Tie one end of the string to one end of the short stick and the other end of the string to the other end of the short stick. The string should be loose in the middle so it hangs down.

Paint with Bubbles

Reuse old bubble cushioning to create cool art.

1. Set up a craft station by laying down a tarp or newspaper. This activity is great for the outdoors since it can get messy.

2. Cut a piece of bubble cushioning down to the same size or smaller than one of the pieces of paper.

3. Paint directly onto the bubble side of the cushioning. You can make an abstract painting, paint a portrait, or anything that comes to mind.

4. When you are finished, flip the bubble cushioning over onto the paper and gently press down. How does it look? What cool creations can you make that incorporate the bubble prints?

What other items can you reuse to create interesting paintings? Think of recycled materials that have unique textures or could act as unusual paintbrushes. Brainstorm three ideas here, and then try them out. Which is your favorite?

Wild Weather

Every type of weather should only appear once in each row, column, and 2 × 3 box. Fill in the squares by drawing or writing the name of each weather type.

BUILD A WIND CHIME

Make a recycled wind chime to hang outdoors.

You Need

- Found objects
- String
- Scissors
- Nail or drill
- Reused hanger
- Decorative items

1. Take a peek in your recycling bin to find items that might make noise when they bump into each other. This could be cleaned tin cans, old metal washers, soda can tabs, utensils, keys, beads, etc.

2. Once you have collected your items, begin tying them to different pieces of string. You can tie several objects to each piece of string, spreading them out along the length of the string. Or you can secure just one object to each piece of string. Just make sure that the objects on different strings hang at the same height so they will bump into each other when jostled by the wind.

3. For objects that do not already have a hole, have an adult add one using the nail or a drill.

4. When you are ready, tie one end of each string to the hanger.

5. Decorate the hanger however you want.

6. Hang it somewhere exposed to wind.

Make a Bug Hotel

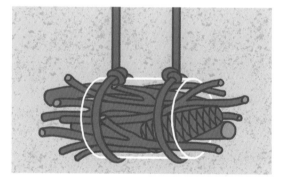

Construct a simple home for insects, and then watch them go about their business.

1. Have an adult help you cut the top and bottom off of the bottle so you are left with a plastic cylinder.

2. Place the cylinder on its side. Arrange your natural items inside the cylinder, filling it tightly so the materials don't slip out.

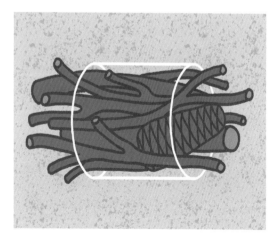

3. Tie a piece of string around one end of the cylinder, knotting it tightly. Do the same thing at the other end. Leave enough string at the ends of both string pieces so you can hang your hotel. The string lengths should be equal so the hotel will hang evenly.

4. Hang your bug hotel somewhere warm and dry. Do you see any bugs over the next few days? Draw them here.

Imagine that there really was a hotel for bugs. What would it look like? Who would the guests be? Write a story about it here.

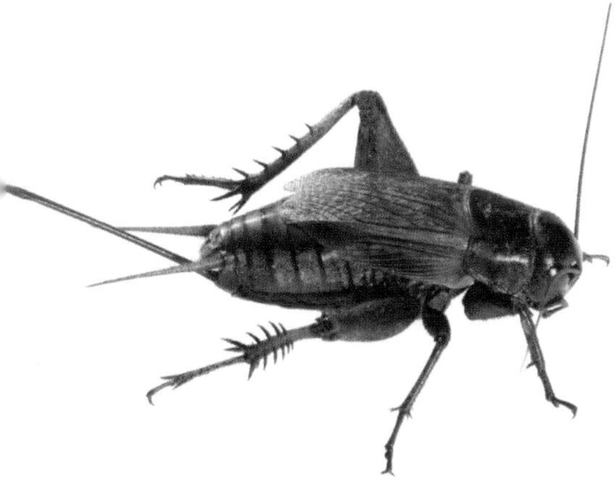

_____

_____

_____

_____

_____

_____

_____

_____

_____

_____

_____

_____

_____

_____

_____

Up Your Neighborhood's Recycling Game

Think about the ways your local community recycles and reduces. Grab an adult and take a stroll to better record your observations. What do you see? What could be better?

_____

_____

_____

_____

_____

What does your local community seem to use the most? What waste do they create? Think about the items you use, or the ways different parts of your community might use different items.

_____

_____

_____

_____

Try to come up with some solutions you think could help cut back on waste or ways to turn the waste into something else.

Take It Further

Have an adult help you reach out to a local community center or council person with your ideas.

Hold an Outdoor Concert

Put on an outdoor concert by creating your own musical instruments from recycled and reused materials.

CARDBOARD BOX GUITAR

You Need

- Recycled cracker or cereal box
- Decorating materials
- Duct tape
- Marker
- Scissors
- Paper towel tube
- Extra-large rubber bands
- Box cutter (optional)

1. Tape all the openings of the box shut. If you want, decorate the box with construction paper or tape.

2. On the front of the box, use the marker to draw or trace a large circle. Have an adult use box cutters or scissors to cut out this circle.

3. Using the paper towel tube, trace another circle onto the top of the box. Cut this one out as well.

4. Using the scissors, make small cuts—about half an inch long—all the way around one end of the tube. Set the tube aside.

5. Wrap four to six rubber bands around the length of the box.

6. Fan out the cut edges of the tube and position the tube against one end of the box so the cut edges lie flat. Use duct tape to secure the tube to this box end.

7. Strum your guitar!

CAN DRUMS

Safety Tip!
Be careful with the edges of a tin can which can be sharp.

You Need

- Large recycled containers like coffee tins or other similar-sized tin cans
- Balloons
- Scissors
- Rubber bands
- Decorating materials

1. Remove the lids from your containers or cans.

2. Cut off the bottom of each balloon so that you can stretch the balloon over the top of a container or can.

3. Secure each balloon in place with a rubber band.

4.. If you want, decorate your drums with construction paper or paint.

....

BOTTLE SHAKERS

You Need

- Recycled plastic bottles
- Gravel, pebbles, old dry rice or beans, recycled beads, or other small noisemaking items
- Decorative materials

1. Fill each bottle about a third to half-way with your noisemaking objects.

2. If you want, decorate the shakers.

CREATE YOUR CONCERT

Grab some friends or family members and create your
own band. Think of some fun band names here.

_____

_____

_____

_____

_____

_____

What songs do you want to play at the concert? Hold some outdoor jam sessions
to practice. When you've decided, list your songs here.

_____

_____

_____

_____

_____

_____

Set up an outdoor stage and a place for your audience to sit. Design it here.

Design some invitations to your outdoor concert! Sketch them here.

For the Birds

See if you can find all the birds listed below in this fun and feathery word search.

Word List

OWL

DOVE

GULL

HAWK

IBIS

SWAN

CRANE

EAGLE

HERON

STORK

FALCON

PARROT

PIGEON

PUFFIN

PELICAN

PENGUIN

FLAMINGO

P E N G U I N X Z

U P I G E O N Z X

F E Z E A G L E J

F L A M I N G O J

I I B I S H A W K

N C R A N E X Y G

Q A P A R R O T U

Q N J S T O R K L

F A L C O N O W L

S W A N X D O V E

MAKE A RECYCLED BIRD FEEDER

1. Have an adult help you cut a hole just big enough to fit your spoon handle on the side of the bottle near the bottom.

2. Slide the handle of one spoon into the bottle through this hole until it reaches the other side. Where it hits the other side, have the adult cut a small hole so the spoon's handle can poke through.

3. Repeat this step with the other spoon about two-thirds of the way up the bottle.

4. Fill the bottle with birdseed and place the cap back on.

5. Tie the string around the neck of the bottle, leaving enough string on both ends for you to hang the feeder.

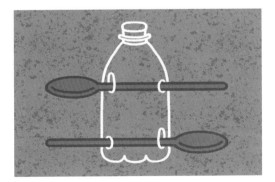

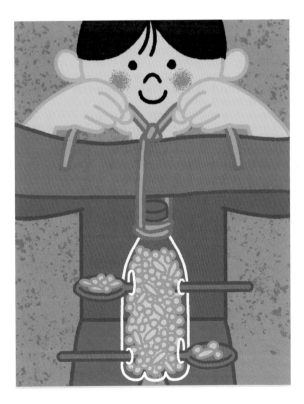

Planter Friend

Bring the outdoors inside with this cute and friendly planter that will green up any space.

1. Cut or tear the paper napkin into small pieces.

2. Cover the plastic bottle with Mod Podge. Stick the napkin pieces on the bottle. Cover with Mod Podge.

3. Cut shapes from the felt to make ears, a nose, and a snout. Glue them to the bottle.

4. Add the wiggle eyes. Add the plant into the bottle. Give it water and sun.

ANSWER KEY

WILD ABOUT NUTS pg. 12

WOMBAT PATH pg. 17

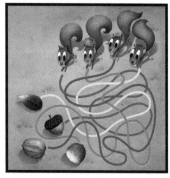

ANIMALS-ABOUT-TOWN pg. 22

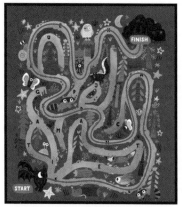

WHAT IS A BAT'S FAVORITE GAME? **FLY-AND-SEEK**

WINDING WATERWAYS pg. 35

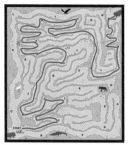

THE **FLORIDA PANTHER** IS AN ENDANGERED EVERGLADES ANIMAL

TERRIFIC TREES pg. 42

BONUS: 32

POND LIFE pg. 50

CAVE QUEST pg. 70

PICNIC FUN pg. 78

A	X	A	2		2	A	A	2	X	X
1	X	2	A		X	A	5	A	X	1
X	X	X	X		A	A	X	X	X	
X	1	A	1		3	X	X	0	X	2
					A	1	X	X	X	A
					1	X	X	1	A	2

JUMP ROPE FUN pg. 128

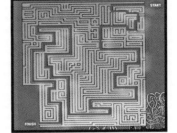

RAINY DAY pg. 88

FISHY FUN pg. 136

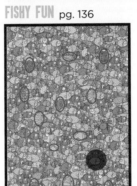

VOLCANO SCIENCE pg. 92

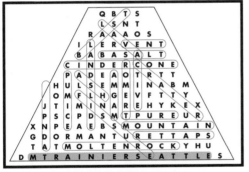

BONUS PUZZLE: **MT. RAINIER, SEATTLE**

WILD WEATHER pg. 144

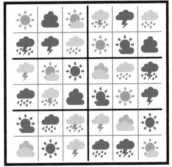

NEIGHBORHOOD HELP pg. 116

FOR THE BIRDS pg. 154

P	E	N	G	U	I	N	X	Z
U	P	I	G	E	O	N	Z	X
F	E	Z	E	A	G	L	E	J
F	L	A	M	I	N	G	O	J
I	N	I	B	I	S	H	A	W	K
N	C	R	A	N	E	X	Y	G
Q	A	P	A	R	R	O	T	U
Q	N	J	S	T	O	R	K	L
F	A	L	C	O	N	O	W	L
S	W	A	N	X	D	O	V	E

CREDITS

Key: GI=Getty Images, IS= iStockphoto, SS=Shutterstock

Published by Highlights Press
815 Church Street
Honesdale, Pennsylvania 18431
ISBN: 978-1-64472-928-1
Manufactured in Dongguan, Guangdong, China
Mfg. 02/2023

First edition
Visit our website at Highlights.com.
10 9 8 7 6 5 4 3 2 1

Produced by WonderLab Group, LLC
Writer: Paige Towler
Designer: Nicole Lazarus
Photo Editor: Annette Kiesow
Copy Editor: Molly Reid
Proofreader: Susan Hom